Library of Congress Control Number: 2023902741
Names: Lubinger, J. David, author| Slivka, Adam, illustrator
Title: The Adventures of Jill, Jake, and Stimlin: Jill And Jake Get A Brother
Summary: Book three, "Jill and Jake Get A Brother," is about how Jill is able to talk
Dad into getting a puppy to keep Jake company while they are in school during the
day. Jill wants to name him Stimlin and they spend the next year searching everywhere
to find their new family member. Will Jill, Jake, and Dad find the perfect "Stimlin" to
make their family bigger and better?

ISBN   978-1-7368466-3-6 (Hardcover)
Subjects: 1. Family Life -Fiction. 2. Unconditional Love- Fiction.   3 Dogs and
puppies- Fiction

The illustrations in this book were created digitally by Adam Slivka
Book design by Adam Slivka

The Adventures of Jill, Jake, and Stimlin

Jill And Jake Get A Brother

Written by
J David Lubinger

Illustrated by
Adam Slivka

Lubinger Press

To Jill, Jake, and Stimlin,
I will love you forever!
-JDL

For Evelyn and Megan
-AS

One day, Jill went up to Dad and asked, "Dad, can we please get another dog to keep Jake company when we are not home?"

Dad said, "That is a good idea. It will make our family even bigger and better."

Jill and Dad loved Jake so much
and wanted him to be happy.

Each weekend, Jill and Dad would take some time to look for the perfect Stimlin, to join the family.

Jill and Dad wanted to get the perfect puppy to spend time with Jake, and make their family even bigger and better.

During that year, they searched here,
and they searched there.

and they searched at animal shelters.

Jill and Dad
searched at dog parks,

and they searched at farms.

Jill and Dad searched
in the newspaper,

It seemed like they searched everywhere.

They saw a lot of dogs and puppies,

Jill wanted to find the perfect
four-legged brother for her and Jake to love.

Jill asked herself,
"Will we ever find the perfect puppy?"

Finally, one day, Jill and Dad found
a cute little white schnoodle,
who looked like a Stimlin,
at the same shelter where they found
Jake!

He had a sweet little face with big brown eyes and scruffy white hair, and he looked happy to see Jill and Dad.

Jill and Dad knew this cute little puppy was the perfect Stimlin!

Jill and Dad went home to get Jake and bring him to meet his new brother, Stimlin.

Jill knew that Jake would have to like Stimlin if they were going to adopt the new puppy.

Jill asked herself, "Will Jake love Stimlin as much as we do?"

When Jake met Stimlin, the two loved each other!

Jill and Dad were so happy that their search had ended, and it brought them to Stimlin.

It was time to bring Stimlin home, so Jill, Jake, Stimlin, and Dad piled into the car and drove home.

The four of them had a fun night playing together, and hugging each other, and feeling happy!

Jill had a smile on her face.

Dad had a smile on his face.

Jake had a smile on his face.

Maybe the happiest of all was Stimlin,
who had found a family to live with,
and a forever home!

CPSIA information can be obtained
at www.ICGtesting.com
Printed in the USA
LVHW071535210323
742157LV00012B/766